Leading with Service

30 Empowering Tips for Turning Customers into Advocates

By Nathan R Mitchell

Leading with Service
30 Empowering Tips for Turning Customers into Advocates
Copyright 2013 by Nathan R Mitchell

ISBN 978-1492222521

Independent Publishing Platform
www.CreateSpace.com

Disclaimer: The advice and strategies contained in this book may not be suitable for your organization. The publisher and author shall not be liable for any loss of profit or other damages that may be incurred by implementing principles and strategies shared herein. You and your organization should consult with a professional where appropriate.

Table of Contents

What Others Are Saying...

Introduction

Leading with Service: *30 Empowering Tips for Turning Customers into Advocates*

About the Author

Order Form

What Others Are Saying...

"Nathan Mitchell's presentations are invaluable. Nathan's genuine demeanor and sincerity connects very well with any audience, and makes his messages powerful. When attending 'Leading With Purpose' at the NALS Professional Development and Education Conference, it was apparent Nathan really cared about giving his audience useful knowledge and insight to become better leaders. As a leader, I gained a new understanding of myself and others. And, in the midst of many changes at NALS, my confidence and abilities to work on successful outcomes for the future was enhanced by his session. Thank you Nathan!" *– Karen McElroy, President-elect NALS, the Association for Legal Professionals*

"Nathan Mitchell is committed to making a difference in the world of business and the lives of others!" *– James Malinchak, Featured on ABC's Hit TV Show Secret Millionaire, Author of 'Millionaire Entrepreneur Secrets,' and Founder of BigMoneySpeaker.com*

—

"Nathan's detailed research and information make it very clear the effects of purposeful-leadership on engagement in the workplace. His training was empowering and insightful. It really opened my eyes."
– Shelia Stephens, Training Specialist, Arvest Bank

"Nathan is an experienced professional dedicated to helping others. His passionate approach to this subject is absolutely inspiring!" *– Dr. Paul Chabot, Founder of Chabot Strategies LLC*

"Nathan knows what it means to overcome adversity and achieve success. He can help you do the same."
– Craig Groeschel, Founder and Senior Pastor of Lifechurch.tv

"Nathan is a breath of fresh air. His seminars provide real-world examples and practical solutions. His experience and passion about his subject matter really shines through." *– Lacey Cline, Organizational Development & Talent Management Professional*

"His insight, passion, and sincerity of purpose is rare in today's business world. If you or your team is looking to go to the next level, you need to call this guy!"
– Clay Clark, U.S. SBA Entrepreneur of the Year

"While at Missouri State University, Nathan studied management and the applications of that knowledge to business situations and problem solving. Solid leadership skills are attributes he has developed through his corporate experience and personal insight." – *Dr. Robert L. Trewatha, Professor Emeritus, Missouri State University*

"I recently attended a workshop with Nathan Mitchell. It was awesome! I came thinking I was going to spend a casual afternoon learning how to sell and grow my business; instead, Nathan showed me the true root for success in my business: Purpose! I've continued to reflect on many of Nathan's ideas since the workshop. Not only is this completely transforming my business; it's taking my team in a whole new direction! I look forward to attending more of Nathan's events!" – *Ashley Walls, Business Owner*

"Nathan Mitchell's purpose in life is to empower other people. If you want to empower your team or your organization at an upcoming event, the next call you need to place is to America's Leading Empowerment Coach™, Nathan R Mitchell!" – *Jim Whitt, Founder of Purpose Unlimited*

Introduction

All organizations should be striving toward a few common goals – 1) discovering and fulfilling their organizational purpose, 2) determining how to best serve the people who purchase their products and services, and 3) fostering a workplace culture with open communication and extraordinary relationships.

If you've read my book *Leading With Purpose: 30 Empowering Tips to Transform Your Organization*, you are well aware of the importance of purposeful-leadership in organizations today. If you haven't read this book, I highly suggest you read this book first, and then return to this one. If you have, congratulations, and welcome to *Leading With Service: 30 Empowering Tips for Turning Customers into Advocates*.

In today's competitive business environment, having loyal customers simply isn't enough. People have too many available choices, and finding the right product or service at the right price is easier than ever before. Today, businesses need advocates; a customer who believes in the products or services a business provides, and who is anxious to tell others about it.

In the business world cash is king, and the customers know it. If customers aren't satisfied with your product or service, approximately 50% of them will leave, start doing business with your competition, and tell seven other people in the process.

—

For one reason or another, when economic times are tough, companies often rethink their customer service strategy. It's easy for every customer to become "treasured" when business is down. Why is this? It doesn't make much sense that a company should take better care of their customers during an economic downturn than they should in any other business climate. Those companies that offer great service all of the time are usually the businesses that end up thriving for years. And with that being said, smart business people and purposeful leaders usually sit at the helm.

It's important for businesses to realize that it isn't necessary to dump large sums of money into developing a new customer service strategy. Customer service also doesn't need to be complicated. Even though some companies, by their horrible service levels alone, may lead you to believe that offering great service is "Rocket Science," it simply isn't true! In fact, great service can often be achieved by doing just a few things extraordinarily well, and for many businesses, service can be improved quite easily.

In "Leading with Service: 30 Empowering Tips for Turning Customers into Advocates," I will help you and your organization identify what's really important to customers today, how you can retain them, and how you can turn them into loyal, business advocates for life by offering extraordinary service that will set you apart from your competition.

Leading with Service

30 Empowering Tips for Turning Customers into Advocates

Tip #1: Treat Your Staff Like Your Best Customer!

"How well do you treat your team members?" It's not a hard question, but more than likely, it's a question we either don't ask very often, or are afraid to ask, because we may not like the answer.

I was a successful, former Fortune 50 Retail Executive and Leader for more than a decade in the pharmaceutical and healthcare industry. One of the many things I learned from those years of experience is this: customer service happens out in the field, on the front lines of business, in areas where many high-level executives and managers simply don't spend enough time.

One thing I can promise you is this: your employees will rarely treat your customers any better than you treat them. So, with that in mind, doesn't it make sense to treat members of your team possibly even better than you treat your very best customer? I think so!

The same courtesies, appreciation, and thankfulness you extend to your loyal customers, should be extend to your employees as well. No one wants to work in an environment where they aren't appreciated, respected, and treated well.

What can you do to serve a member of your team today?

Today's Service Intention

"The goal as a company is to have customer service that is not just the best but legendary."
– Sam Walton, Founder of Wal-Mart

What 2-3 action items are you going to do today to better serve your customer?

1.

2.

3.

Tip #2: Simply Say "Thank You!"

While attending a seminar for professional speakers hosted by *ABC's Secret Millionaire*, James Malinchak, I heard him say, "Little Hinges Swing Big Doors." In other words, the simple things matter. And one of the simplest things we can do as business owners is simply say "Thank You" to our customers.

I've met many sales professionals through the years who have told me they lose a certain percentage of their customers each year based on price alone. In others words, some people are willing to leave for a measly $50 a year. As someone who has a lot of experience in marketing, I see this as a communication problem, not a price issue.

I've been a client of some of these sales professionals myself, and once I signed on the dotted line, I no longer heard from them – never received a hand-written "Thank You" note, or even a phone call.

Friends, giving thanks shouldn't be reserved for new clients, or for holidays. It's not hard to say "Thank You" in business, and sometimes that's all your customers really want's to hear. They want to know you appreciate and value their business.

Remember, "little hinges swing big doors." The simple things really do matter.

Today's Service Intention

"Your most unhappy customers are your greatest source of learning." **– Bill Gates**

What 2-3 action items are you going to do today to better serve your customer?

1.

2.

3.

Tips #3: Be an Active Listener

Have you ever dealt with an upset customer? If you've been in business long enough, or you service a large number of clients, my guess is you have. I know I've had my fair share! The retail industry can be notorious for upset customers, and I spent a significant portion of my professional career in it. Obviously, we like to keep these types of situations to a minimum, but again, if you are in business long enough, you will more than likely experience the frustration shared by an upset customer.

The important thing to keep in mind is this: customers want to be heard. Don't get me wrong. I'm not saying you won't have to make things right, but start by being an active listener. Be empathetic of their situation. They will feel so much better about continuing to do business with you, and more than likely they will tell you exactly what they want. And that makes it pretty easy to over-deliver.

The last thing you should do is hide behind your company's policies and procedures. The customer doesn't care what your employee handbook says regarding how you should handle their situation. They just want to know that you are willing to make it right, and you can only accomplish that if you are paying attention to their needs!

Today's Service Intention

"It is not the employer who pays the wages. Employers only handle the money. It is the customer who pays the wages." **– Henry Ford**

What 2-3 action items are you going to do today to better serve your customer?

1.

2.

3.

Tip #4: Focus on What You Can Do

Nothing aggravates a customer more than telling them there's nothing you can do to help them. In today's ultra-competitive business environment where customers have so many options available to them, organizations must commit to handling complaints in such a way that lead the customer to believe that your company is a great organization to work with!

If you were to seriously evaluate the current level of service throughout your organization, does the way you operate leave the customer thinking this about your company?

When dealing with difficult customer service situations, Instead of telling a customer there's nothing you can do to help them, focus on what you can do! This is so important, it's worth repeating: always focus on what you can do, not on what you cannot do! Regardless of what your policies and procedures state, there is always a solution. It may not always be what the customer wants, but it's better than nothing.

When you focus on what you can do, there's still a possibility you will be able to resolve their issue. When possible, offer more than one solution. Customers feel empowered when you give them a choice, and more than likely they will come back to do business with you again.

Today's Service Intention

"Spend a lot of time talking to customers face to face. You'd be amazed how many companies don't listen to their customers." **– Ross Perot**

What 2-3 action items are you going to do today to better serve your customer?

1.

2.

3.

Tip #5: Handle Complaints Quickly

Have you ever walked in to a new day at the office only to be bombarded with news of a customer who had an undesirable experience with your company, and they want to talk to YOU? If you've been in management long enough, more than likely you have. In situations like this it's easy to put off these difficult conversations when the customer isn't in your place of business staring you in the face. It's easy to push the note or news aside and say to ourselves, "I'll get to it later."

Most people don't like to have difficult conversations. And most people don't like confrontation; however, in the worlds of management and leadership, it comes with the territory. Early on in my professional career as a Retail Executive, I remember saying to myself, "I'll give this one a couple of days; perhaps that will give them an opportunity to cool off before I reach out to them." The problem is, when I did get around to calling, they often wouldn't take my call nor return it. In other words, they had gotten over it and moved on, and I missed a critical opportunity to make things right.

Don't make the same mistakes I made early on in my career. Customer complaints need to be handled as quickly as possible while the experience is fresh on your customer's mind, and yours too. So, pick up the phone, write the letter, and click send on the email. You will be so grateful you did!

Today's Service Intention

"If you do build a great experience, customers tell each other about that. Word of mouth is very powerful." – **Jeff Benzos, CEO of Amazon**

What 2-3 action items are you going to do today to better serve your customer?

1.

2.

3.

Tip #6: Keep Your Word

As business owners, managers, and leaders we prefer that our customers are loyal to our products and services versus those of our competitors. Believe it or not, your customers expect the same kind of loyalty - and that all starts with keeping your promises.

Make sure you always honor your word, and honor your commitment to your existing customers and clientele. If you were to break down customer service to its simplest form, this is what customer service is all about: keeping your promises.

It's important to note that keeping your word and honoring your promises doesn't start with the customer. It starts by keeping your word and honoring your promises to those in your organization; the ones who are out in the field interacting with your customers on a daily basis. Remember, earlier in the book, I mentioned that you should treat members of your team as good as (if not better than) the way you treat your best customer!

Your people are the face of your organization. They are the backbone of your sales and revenue. If you don't keep your word to them, they won't do the same for those who drive your bottom line!

Today's Service Intention

"The customer experience is the next competitive battleground." **– Jerry Gregoire, CIO, Dell Computers**

What 2-3 action items are you going to do today to better serve your customer?

1.

2.

3.

Tip #7: Come from a Position of Serving

If you've read my book "Leading with Purpose: 30 Empowering Tips to Transform Your Organization," you know that I discussed the importance of servant-leadership in organizations today. When we think of servant-leadership, we typically think of it from an internal perspective. In other words, the leadership style within an organization. However, we should approach customer service in much the same way!

As servant leaders, one of your primary goals should be to make sure that your customer's needs are top priority and that they are being served, always! As you and I both know, excellent customer service in foundational to a company's survival. It amazes me how many companies today fail to exceed expectations in this area of their business. Excellent customer service must be a priority for every business and for every team member in the organization, regardless of position and rank - there are no exceptions!

Philippians Chapter 2 tells us "Agree with each other, love each other, be deep-spirited friends. Don't push your way to the front; don't sweet-talk your way to the top. Put yourself aside, and help others get ahead. Don't be obsessed with getting your own advantage. Forget yourselves long enough to lend a helping hand," (The Message).

How will you serve someone today?

Today's Service Intention

"Customer satisfaction if worthless. Customer loyalty is priceless." **– Jeffrey Gitomer**

What 2-3 action items are you going to do today to better serve your customer?

1.

2.

3.

Tip #8: Empower Your People!

I'm sure you have heard the old adage, "People are your greatest asset!" The truth is empowered people are your greatest asset. You can have an organization filled with the smartest executives, key leadership, and several hundred team members, but if they aren't empowered in their positions, being efficient and productive in their jobs, and serving the needs and wants of your loyal customers and clients, having a large group of team members is futile.

Looking back over the past decade, there have been a number of large companies that have ultimately gone out of business due to the lack of leadership and sound business ethics at the top of the organization. Simply being in business doesn't equate to having the right people on the bus. And as leaders and managers, you have control over that, not to mention, it's your responsibility! And it all starts with employee empowerment.

Studies show that empowered employees are more effective in their work, they are more productive, and they serve the needs of the customers better than those who aren't. They also tend to be more loyal, and stay with your organization longer, thus decreasing your employee turnover. At the end of the day, empowered employees make customers want to return again and again to do business with you. Disempowered employees run them off!

Today's Service Intention

"Quality in a service or product is not what you put into it. It is what the client or customer gets out of it." **– Peter Drucker**

What 2-3 action items are you going to do today to better serve your customer?

1.

2.

3.

Tip #9: Go the Extra Mile

As a former, successful retail executive and leader with a Fortune 50 company, I'm well aware that some team members will focus on their job description and that's it. In other words, they will do what is expected of them and nothing more. Unfortunately, many organizations treat their customer service in much the same way. They will do the bare minimum to meet the needs of the customer, and nothing more.

Customer service isn't rocket science, and believe it or not, customers don't expect as much as you think they do. It doesn't take a lot to go the extra mile, and do those things your competitors aren't willing to do! Your customers work hard for their money just like you do, and more often than not they exercise great caution in how they spend it. Your staff should always be willing to lend a helping hand and to exceed your customers' expectations.

So with that in mind, here are a few tips on how to go the extra mile with your customers:

1) Be polite and smile often!
2) Ask the customer what they want, and then do it!
3) Keep your word by honoring your promises!
4) Be empathetic of their situation and their needs!
5) Surprise them by delivering more than they expect!
6) Always follow-up

Today's Service Intention

"Customers don't expect you to be perfect. They do expect you to fix things when they go wrong." **– Donald Porter, V.P. British Airways**

What 2-3 action items are you going to do today to better serve your customer?

1.

2.

3.

Tip #10: Treat Your Customers Like Individuals

Consider for a moment two companies that offer the exact same product or service - how does one differentiate itself from the other? All else equal, the level of service is usually the differentiating factor. In today's high-tech world, one of the easiest ways for organizations to do this is to treat their customers like individuals. Think about this: technology has given us the ability to reach more people than ever. With that being said, what's the result? In all actuality, we live in a High-Reach, Low-Touch world. Technology has given us the ability to reach people easier, but it hasn't helped us connect with them. When it comes to service, the ability to connect is critical, and that is achieved by treating them like individuals, and building the relationship.

When was the last time your wrote a handwritten "Thank You" note to a customer? More than likely, it's been a while. Most organizations and business owners don't do this. And I'm not talking about the cheesy birthday card that is anything but personal that every single customer in your database receives. The key to treating customers like individuals is simple: it's personalized attention! Find ways to deliver a differentiated, personalized customer experience, and you will blow the doors off the competition!

Today's Service Intention

"There is a spiritual aspect to our lives – when we give we receive – when a business does something good for somebody, that somebody feels good about them!" **– Ben Cohen, Ben & Jerry's**

What 2-3 action items are you going to do today to better serve your customer?

1.

2.

3.

Tip #11: Who Are Your Top 10 Customers?

Organizations must turn a profit to stay in business. Many companies will spend thousands, hundreds of thousands, and even millions of dollars to reach new customers in order to generate sales. The truth is many businesses and corporations are unable to invest this kind of money in their marketing.

I regularly consult with small to medium-sized businesses, and one of the things I talk about often is the fact that it is much easier, and much more cost-effective, to get additional business from existing customers than it is to acquire a new one. In all reality, generating profitable revenue growth through a company's current customer base is one of the most overlooked marketing opportunities.

The first step in taking advantage of this opportunity is to know who your top customers are. Fox example, if you are an entrepreneur, who are your top ten or top one hundred customers? Once you identify them, ask yourself "when was the last time we reached out to these customers?" If you don't consistently reach out, you have no idea whether or not their needs have changed.

So, with this in mind, how are you going to reach out to your existing customers starting today? It's an instrumental piece of great customer service!

Today's Service Intention

"The more you engage with customers the clearer things become and the easier it is to determine what you should be doing." **– John Russell, Harley Davidson**

What 2-3 action items are you going to do today to better serve your customer?

1.

2.

3.

Tip #12: Keep in Touch!

Part of getting repeat business from existing customers involves staying in touch. The key to staying in touch is to do so in a unique and memorable way! To piggyback on what I addressed earlier, you've got to know who your top customers and clients are. Once you've identified them, ask yourself, "How can I deliver value to these individuals in a memorable way that will differentiate me from other business owners?" The key is to follow-through. The fact that you will do this alone will set you apart from many other organizations and business owners.

If you've done a good job of getting to know your customers, and you've also done a good job of logging it in your customer database, this should be relatively easy for you. For example, if you have a client who is a big sports fan, consider sending them a complimentary gift subscription to one of the top sports publications. Ten or $20 is a minimal investment to deliver value to a long-term customer who may tell ten to twenty of their close friends about you and the value you bring to the marketplace.

Remember, keeping in touch is all about being memorable, and delivering value to your top customers in a unique and meaningful way. I promise; they will appreciate you!

Today's Service Intention

"Being on par in terms of price and quality only gets you into the game. Service wins the game."
– Tony Allesandra

What 2-3 action items are you going to do today to better serve your customer?

1.

2.

3.

Tip #13: Read What Your Customers Read

Wouldn't customer service be so much easier at times if we could read our customers' minds? Unfortunately, despite major advancements in technology, this still isn't possible. However, depending on your industry and the number of customers or clients you serve, there are some things you can do to have a greater understanding of your customer's world.

As a business coach and management consultant one of the things I do is study up on the industries of my clientele. This may or may not apply to your business or your industry, but if it does, one of the things you can do is read what your customers read. In other words, learn their language! Here are a few tips on how you can stay informed:

1. Visit relevant online forums and discussion boards
2. Read books related to their industry
3. Visit their website and stay informed
4. Read relevant magazines and trade journals
5. If the write, read it
6. Don't be afraid to ask

The bottom line is simple: don't assume you know everything about your client, and never assume you know what they want.

Today's Service Intention

"You'll never have a product or price advantage again. They can be easily duplicated, but a strong customer service culture can't be copied." **– Jerry Fritz**

What 2-3 action items are you going to do today to better serve your customer?

1.

2.

3.

Tip #14: Ask for Feedback, and then Reward It!

Businesses who have happy customers simply make more money, period! There's simply no way you can argue against this point. So far in this book, I've addressed a number of different things that can help you as a business owner keep your customers happy. The problem, however, is how do you know if your customers are satisfied or dissatisfied with the product or service you offer? Simply ask them!

Asking for customer feedback is a great way to gain invaluable insight into your daily business operations. There are a number of different ways you can do this, including surveys, phone calls, and even the use of social media. The important thing to remember is this: once your customers have given you feedback, find ways to reward them. Perhaps a $20 off coupon on their next visit will suffice. The value of the reward doesn't matter nearly as much as the fact that you are involving the customer in the day-to-day decisions of your business, and even more importantly, that you are taking the information to heart and using it to improve. Begin acquiring feedback starting today!

Today's Service Intention

"Know what your customers want most and what your company does best. Focus on where those two meet." **– Kevin Stirtz**

What 2-3 action items are you going to do today to better serve your customer?

1.

2.

3.

Tip #15: Identify Your Ideal Service Model

When it comes to customer service, as a business owner, one of your goals should be to maximize customer satisfaction and minimize customer dissatisfaction. With this goal in mind, what customer service model do you currently have in place to ensure this happens?

Customer service models should include several different things: 1) strategies for gathering feedback, 2) strategies for handling and retaining dissatisfied customers, and 3) strategies for meeting your customers' needs!

Before developing your customer service model, the first thing you must do is define what customer service means to your organization. In other words, what does great customer service look like for you? I recommend outlining all aspects of your customer service strategy. Review these against the purpose of your organization to ensure strategic alignment, and then begin implementing them into your organization's customer service policies and procedures.

Today's Service Intention

"Loyal customers, they don't just come back, they don't simply recommend you, that insist that their friends to business with you." – **Chip Bell**

What 2-3 action items are you going to do today to better serve your customer?

1.

2.

3.

Tip #16: Take Responsibility!

For every customer that lets you know they have had an unsatisfactory experience with your organization, there are often many others who haven't made you aware. Most customers will not come right out and tell you that they've had a bad experience - instead, they will just leave and not come back. Oh by the way, they will usually tell at least seven other people that they've had a bad experience with your company in the process.

So, here's my point: when a customer complains, welcome the opportunity to take the feedback and improve. More importantly, own up to the shortcomings in your service and take responsibility. More often than not the customer simply wants to be heard. When you take responsibility customers appreciate it, and they feel like their opinion matters!

So, when a customer complains, recognize it as the golden opportunity it is. Take responsibility, make things right for the customer, and commit to improving on what you've learned! You will be so grateful you did!

Today's Service Intention

"Make a customer, not a sale." – **Katherine Barchetti**

What 2-3 action items are you going to do today to better serve your customer?

1.

2.

3.

Tips #17: Keep an Eye on the Competition

When it comes to customer service, what do you know about your competition? What specific things are they doing to win the hearts of customers? Is their customer service inferior to yours, or is it better? Do you even know?

As necessary as it is for organizations to keep an eye on what the competition is doing, many organizations aren't as aware as they should be with regards to what the competition is doing to reach, service, and retain customers.

Taking the time necessary to watch your competitors can reap huge dividends in both the short-term and the long-term. It gives you the opportunity to learn from their strengths and their weaknesses, as well as gives you additional ideas on how your business can be more unique by serving the customer better.

Don't allow your organization to become complacent by falling into the "we're the best" trap. Keep an eye on the competition, learn from others outside your industry, and make a commitment to lifelong learning and improvement! Your customers will thank you for it!

Today's Service Intention

"Make your product easier to buy than your competition, or you will find your customers buying from them, not you." – **Mark Cuban**

What 2-3 action items are you going to do today to better serve your customer?

1.

2.

3.

Tip #18: Watch Your Best Staff Members Serve

In the previous tip, I addressed the importance of keeping an eye on your competition. Now I want to address the importance of observing existing members of your team. Who are the top three team members in your organization that offer the best possible service "hands down?" Hopefully, you already know who they are. If you don't, start analyzing the service of your team members now, and identify them as soon as possible.

Members of your team who offer extraordinary service are a great asset to your company. Not only do they already serve your customers well, but they can also teach others to do the same. The question is, are you using them in this capacity? It isn't always necessary to bring in an outside trainer for your organization to brush up on it s customer service skills. Sometimes you already have the personnel you need to be effective. Not only will members of your organization be more open-minded to "in house" training, but the people you have chosen to give the training will feel more empowered in their roles.

So, with this in mind, are you going to make the commitment to learn from team members in your organization who already know how to serve your customer best? You should!

Today's Service Intention

"If you work just for money, you'll never make it, but if you love what you're doing and you always put the customer first, success will be yours." **– Ray Krock**

What 2-3 action items are you going to do today to better serve your customer?

1.

2.

3.

Tip #19: Little Things Produce Great Results

I've spent a lot of time through the years reading and listening to top business experts and motivational gurus. One of those individuals who have had a profound impact on my work is Tony Robbins. One of the things I learned from Tony is this: wherever your focus goes, energy flows. When you begin to make customer service an important focus in the day-to-day operations of your business, over time you will begin to see extraordinary results in your operation.

As I mentioned earlier in the book, "Little Hinges Swing Big Doors." More often than not it's the little things that make a difference. And it's the little things that you do on a daily basis that over time will reap huge dividends for you.

For example, if you are looking to build a strong customer-focused business, start by hiring the right people whose goals and ambitions are in alignment with the purpose of your organization. And secondly, focus on improving your organizational culture. No, these things cannot be done overnight; however, when you put the small, simple things, in place day after day after day that improve these areas, before you know it, you will have a business with long-term advocates, not just satisfied customers.

Today's Service Intention

"Customer service is just a day in, day out, ongoing, never ending, unremitting, persevering, compassionate, type of activity."
- Leon Gorman, CEO LL Bean

What 2-3 action items are you going to do today to better serve your customer?

1.

2.

3.

Tip #20: Ask "How Will This Affect My Customer?"

As business owners, leaders, and managers we face hard decisions almost daily. Whether those decisions involve business strategy, marketing, finances, or personnel issues, we should always ask ourselves the following question: "How will the decisions I make today affect the customers of the business." Unfortunately, we don't always ask this question, or even think this way; however, it's the customers who ultimately drive the bottom line in your business. So, with this in mind, what decisions are on your plate today, and how will the decisions you make affect those who give you their hard-earned money.

When it comes to decisions that directly affect our customers, nothing is more important than the people we hire. It's hard for an organization to drive satisfactory service with the wrong people on the bus.

When I was in the corporate sector, and was responsible for hiring hundreds of employees over the span of my career, I made a concerted effort to hire the smile and train the task. Yes, I was guilty of hiring people who "on paper," weren't the ideal candidate for the job, but their personality and their ability to relate with others made up for it and more. That's the reason why one of the locations I managed was selected "Store of the Year" within my district for customer service. What decisions are you making today?

Today's Service Intention

"Every company's greatest assets are its customers, because without customers there is no company." **– Michael LaBoeuf**

What 2-3 action items are you going to do today to better serve your customer?

1.

2.

3.

Tip #21: Complaints = Opportunities to Improve

It has been estimated that nearly nine out of every ten upset customers will not complain about their poor experience with a company. In other words, they simply move on and take their business elsewhere. This may be hard to believe, but think for a moment about your own behavior. Do you bother? The majority of us don't! We simply walk away.

My point is that as a leader in your organization, you have an opportunity to make things right only about ten-percent of the time. When customers are upset with the level of service you are providing, their complaints should be welcomed, not viewed as a nuisance! Complaints are really opportunities for you business to improve. Customer complaints can help your organization:

- Evaluate your current level of customer service
- See customer service situations from a different perspective
- Improve customer satisfaction over the long-term
- Identify weaknesses in your customer service strategy and correct them
- Turn customers into loyal, business advocates for life!

Today's Service Intention

"Excellent firms don't believe in excellence – only in constant improvement and constant change." **– Tom Peters**

What 2-3 action items are you going to do today to better serve your customer?

1.

2.

3.

Tip #22: Think and Act Like Disney

"If you can dream it, you can do it." That's one of the many great statements Walt Disney left us with before he passed away at the age of 65 in 1966 from lung cancer. Another good one is: "Get a good idea, and stay with it. Dog it, and work at it until it's done, and done right!"

A couple of years back, we took the family to Disney World for a week. Although I had been there several times as a child myself, I don't I think fully appreciated the experience at those ages. Now, as a grown man with a passion for business and service, it's literally breathtaking to take it all in. From the moment you enter the theme park grounds, the experience and the service is extraordinary.

Here is what I observed regarding Disney's service during our trip: the people are very friendly; they make the customer feel appreciated; despite the amount of foot-traffic, the parks are nearly spotless; and everything is "show ready!"

There's no doubt in my mind that Disney may have the best customer service training in any industry. I highly recommend that you study what they do, and try your best to replicate it for your own organization!

Despite Disney's passing, they still "Dog it, and work at it until it's done, and done right!"

Today's Service Intention

"Friendly makes sales – and friendly generates repeat business." **– Jeffrey Gitomer**

What 2-3 action items are you going to do today to better serve your customer?

1.

2.

3.

Tip #23: Learn From Your Successes & Failures

How many times have you heard, "You need to learn from your mistakes?" We hear this all the time in one way or another. It would be hard to argue that it hasn't become cliché. I'm not saying that there isn't value in learning from our shortcomings with clients, our failure to meet their expectations, etc., but to some degree it is a misconception, because it's only one piece of the puzzle when striving for improvement.

When we learn from our mistakes, hopefully we learn what not to do again. The most important thing is that we actually follow-through by not doing that same thing twice. Unfortunately, I know I've made the same mistake twice; sometimes more than twice! So, how much value is there in that: sometimes a lot; sometimes a little.

My point here is that we should also learn from our successes with customers, because when we learn from our successes at least we know what works, and you can then repeat it over and over again, usually with satisfactory results.

And you never know, you may even do it better the next time!

Today's Service Intention

"Service, in short, is not what you do, but who you are. It is a way of living that you need to bring to everything you do, if you are to bring it to your customer interactions." — **Betsy Sanders**

What 2-3 action items are you going to do today to better serve your customer?

1.

2.

3.

Tip #24: Focus on the Relationship

I've been fortunate to have the opportunity to teach business at the college level for quite some time. It's great having the ability to teach and coach others even when I'm not working with business clients, speaking, or giving leadership training for organizations or associations.

One thing I always tell my business students is this: if I had to summarize what it takes to succeed in business in one word, that word would be *relationships*! That's really the foundation for business success.

When I do training on customer service, I always talk about the importance of focusing on and building the customer relationship. You see, losing a customer is the absolute worst thing that can happen for an organization, especially in today's market conditions. That's why it's so important to focus on customer retention and building the customer relationship. Here are a few suggestions on how you can do just that:

- Over-communicate! Don't just call to make a sale.
- Implement a customer-loyalty program.
- Emphasize the human factor. Do you know all of your customers by name? And...
- Always be willing to work with them. Make adjustments as necessary to meet their needs.

Today's Service Intention

"Here is a simple but powerful rule: always give people more than what they expect to get."
– Nelson Boswell

What 2-3 action items are you going to do today to better serve your customer?

1.

2.

3.

Tip #25: Commit to Training & Development

An organization is only as good as the people who lead it and the people who work for it. Furthermore, an organization's customer service is only as good as the level of service ability of those who provide it. That's why ongoing training and development is so important.

I get excited when I receive a phone call from a company or association that wants to bring me in to do training for them, because that tells me they understand the importance of ongoing training and development.

Smart companies understand that market conditions, the workplace, as well as the workforce are constantly in flux, and that in order to keep pace with changing conditions, staff members must also continue to evolve themselves and acquire new skills.

The key here is to make sure the training and development you offer is effective. The last thing you want to do is simply offer some training program to simply "check the box." Believe me, your staff members will know the difference!

In addition to improved customer service, a commitment to ongoing training and development will make your employees better prepared to meet the organization's goals; they will have improved customer interaction and service; employee morale will be higher; and you will experience decreased turnover and increased productivity!

Today's Service Intention

"Customers today want the very most and the very best for the least amount of money, and on the best terms. Only the individuals and companies that provide absolutely excellent products and services at absolutely excellent prices will survive." **– Brian Tracy**

What 2-3 action items are you going to do today to better serve your customer?

1.

2.

3.

Tip #26: Develop a Customer-First Culture

My good friend and fellow consultant, Jim Whitt, says an organization's purpose must be positive, powerful, simple and *serving*. If an organization is going to survive over the long-term, it must have a customer-first culture.

Customer service has to be built into an organization's DNA. Many companies have mission statements that in one way or another emphasize the importance of customer service, but much like Jim, I prefer statements of purpose!

I have a consulting client in the public accounting industry. The organization just doesn't do bookkeeping, payroll accounting, budgeting and tax returns. No, they do much more than that! They *Relieve Financial Stress*! Notice how their purpose is positive, powerful, simple and *serving*. Their purpose helps them drive a customer-first culture. Every employee in the organization knows and understands it, and goes out of their way to deliver that outcome.

So, is the mission of your organization focused on putting the needs of the customer first? Does it show your commitment to building a "customer-first culture?" Or, is your mission focused on driving shareholder wealth and bottom-line profitability? Allow me to let you in on a little secret: focus on putting the needs of the customer first, and the others will follow!

Today's Service Intention

"Statistics suggest that when customers complain, business owners and managers ought to get excited about it. The complaining customer represents a huge opportunity for more business." **– Zig Ziglar**

What 2-3 action items are you going to do today to better serve your customer?

1.

2.

3.

Tip #27: Hold a Customer Appreciation Event

Do you find ways to make your customers feel appreciated? Sometimes it can be difficult. I mean, what's the best way to show them that you care and appreciate them without breaking the bank at the same time? One of the ways you can do this is by holding a Customer Appreciation Event. And the good news is that they work in just about any industry!

One of the things I like most about Customer Appreciation Events is that they also serve as another great way to market your products and services. What better way to introduce a new product line or new service than after you have showed your appreciation and delivered a ton of value?

Another thing you can do when having a Customer Appreciation Event, is to allow your customers to bring guests along with them. Yes, this will add to the cost of your event; however, it's a pretty easy way to get additional business through customer referrals. More often than not your clients won't bring someone along with them who isn't a good fit for the product or service you offer, or who hasn't expressed an interest in possibly doing business with you.

Depending on how elaborate you make your event, the costs of holding one can vary greatly; however, over the long-term, the benefits to your bottom-line far outweigh the costs of doing them.

Today's Service Intention

"If you don't genuinely like your customers, chances are they won't buy." – **Thomas Watson, former CEO of IBM**

What 2-3 action items are you going to do today to better serve your customer?

1.

2.

3.

Tip #28: Smile Often

Smiling often has to be the most simple, easiest tip in the whole book. I'm not saying it's the easiest one to pull off and to make happen in your organization, but the concept isn't hard at all. If you are part of an organization that treats your employees well and has a customer-first culture, this will be easier for you than those organizations that don't.

When I was a Retail Executive with a Fortune 50 company, we had a list of seven principles, or things we should do on a daily basis, to provide the best service possible to our customers. The number one thing we were asked to do was to smile at every single customer that we came into contact with in the store.

People say that smiling requires the engagement of fewer muscles in the face than frowning does. So, not only is it easier to pull-off, but smiling has the potential to brighten your customer's day. In fact, some studies suggest that smiling has monetary value in the world of business. In other words, people are more likely to do business with you, because they trust you more when you have a friendly face.

So, find a way to smile often, especially in front of your customers. Not only will it make you and your customers happier, but it is also something that you can implement right away that involves absolutely zero additional work! Start spreading more joy today!

Today's Service Intention

"People expect good service, but few are willing to give it." – **Robert Gateley**

What 2-3 action items are you going to do today to better serve your customer?

1.

2.

3.

Tip# 29: Give Them the Unexpected!

With all of the advancements in the world around us, customers have come to expect great products and services. As a business owner, the real connection with the customer occurs when you find a way to go above and beyond – not only meeting their expectations, but also exceeding them!

I've made a conscious effort throughout this book to emphasize over and over the importance of doing the little things right. It really is the small things that make the difference. Few companies find a way to exceed customers' expectations regularly, but when it does happen, it's easy to turn what could be an everyday, ordinary visit into an extraordinary one!

As business owners, managers and leaders, we aren't really any different than those we serve; let's face it, we are also consumers. Think of the times throughout your life when a company far exceeded your expectations. What did they do? What was it exactly that "knocked your socks off?" Can you find a way to replicate it in your own business?

When I talk about giving customers the unexpected, it doesn't have to be anything major. Sometimes, it's the small actions that can transform their experience with you into a memorable one. It's also the small things that create long-term customer loyalty. In other words, it's how you can turn everyday customers into loyal advocates for your organization.

Today's Service Intention

"Do what you do so well that they will want to see it again and bring their friends." – **Walt Disney**

What 2-3 action items are you going to do today to better serve your customer?

1.

2.

3.

Tip #30: Create an Environment of Excellence

The last thing I want to cover is this: the importance of creating an environment of excellence throughout your organization! This covers everything from your culture, to your business practices and strategies, to the way your treat your customers.

In the world of business we get what we expect. If you don't expect excellence, more than likely you won't achieve it; however, if you set your expectations high, regularly measure your progress, and make adjustments along the way, you will improve you're your service levels dramatically.

Creating an environment of excellence begins with asking, "Where do we want this company to be, and where are we currently?" It's hard to get to where you want to be if you don't first know where you are.

Secondly, clearly define what excellence means to you, and then do everything you can to foster it on a daily basis. Be as detailed as possible. Set timelines for your goals, and benchmark your standards against those of your competition! You can then put systems, procedures and expectations into place to achieve the results you desire.

Excellence doesn't happen overnight, but it does happen by doing little things right over and over again. Little things done right every single day result in the accomplishment of extraordinary things over time.

Today's Service Intention

"Under-promise and over-deliver." – **Toby Bloomberg**

What 2-3 action items are you going to do today to better serve your customer?

1.

2.

3.

About the Author

Nathan R Mitchell is America's Leading Empowerment Coach, and the founder of Clutch Consulting. He is an experienced business and leadership development coach, author, and speaker. Nathan helps career professionals, executives, and business owners become better leaders and become more engaged in the workplace by finding purpose, meaning, and fulfillment in the work they do.

He holds a Bachelor of Science Degree in Entrepreneurship, an MBA from Missouri State University, and Certifications in Professional Coaching, Behaviors, and Motivators Analysis. After graduating from college, he took an operations management position with a Fortune 50 company where he had eleven years of success before leaving to pursue other endeavors.

In 2010 he started Clutch Consulting with one simple purpose: "Growing Businesses and Empowering People." Nathan loves affecting change, mentoring others, creating new ideas and innovative ways of doing things, giving others perspective, and helping companies have better bottom lines.

If you are interested in consulting, training programs, workshops, or speaking engagements for your organization, simply contact Nathan R Mitchell:

Phone: 918.851.7246
Online: NathanRMitchell.com
ClutchConsulting.net

Sign up for Nathan's FREE, Weekly E-Newsletter at NathanRMitchell.com

Book Order Form

If you would like to order **Nathan Mitchell's** book *Leading with Service: 30 Empowering Tips for Turning Customers into Advocates* for members of your team or organization, fill out the form below and mail to:

Nathan R Mitchell
PO Box 2818
Broken Arrow, OK 74013
918.851.7246

Name: _____

Address: _____

City: _____

State: _____

Zip Code: _____

Phone: _____

Email: _____

Continued on Next Page...

Type of Card: _____

Credit Card Number: _____

Expiration Date: _____

3-Digit Security Code: _____

Quantity of Books You Would Like: _____

Total Price: ($14.95 x Qty. Ordered) _____

TOTAL PRICE INCLUDES S&H
THANK YOU FOR YOUR ORDER!!!

Company Checks Are Also Accepted...

Please allow 3-4 weeks for delivery. Should it take longer, we will contact you as soon as possible.

Made in the USA
Charleston, SC
12 September 2013